Dedicated to the Royal Philharmonic Society

SYMPHONY No. 9
IN E MINOR
By
R. VAUGHAN WILLIAMS

MOVEMENTS

I	Moderato maestoso	page	1
II	Andante sostenuto	„	40
III	Scherzo (allegro pesante)	„	72
IV	Andante tranquillo	„	129

OXFORD UNIVERSITY PRESS
Music Department
44 CONDUIT STREET, LONDON, W.1

Made in Great Britain

ORCHESTRATION

2 Flutes	2 Saxophones in E♭
Piccolo (3rd Flute)	Saxophone in B♭
2 Oboes	4 Horns in F
Cor Anglais	Flügel Horn in B♭
2 Clarinets in B♭	2 Trumpets in B♭
Bass Clarinet in B♭	3 Trombones
2 Bassoons	Tuba
Double Bassoon	Timpani

Percussion:
- Glockenspiel
- Xylophone
- Side Drum
- Tenor Drum
- Bass Drum
- Cymbals
- Triangle
- Very Large (Deep) Gong
- Tam-tam
- Deep Bells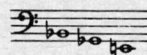

2 Harps   Celesta   Strings

Of the "extra" instruments the 1st E♭ Saxophone is indispensable—the 2nd E♭ and 3rd B♭ Saxophones are nearly so, but in the case of absolute necessity these may be dispensed with by playing the cues chiefly in Clarinet and Bassoon parts.

The Flügel Horn is also very important, but if such an instrument is absolutely not to be had the part may be played in the *tutti* on a 3rd Trumpet, some solo passages being cued in for 1st Trumpet or 1st Horn.

The Flügel Horn part must *never* be played on a Cornet; also the conductor must make sure that the player uses a real Flügel Horn mouthpiece.

Duration 30 minutes

Orchestral material, including large-size scores, is available on hire.

This work was given its first performance at the Royal Philharmonic Society's concert in London on 2nd April, 1958, conducted by Sir Malcolm Sargent.

SYMPHONY No. 9 IN E MINOR

Dedicated to the Royal Philharmonic Society

R. VAUGHAN WILLIAMS

© Copyright, 1958, by the Oxford University Press, London

OXFORD UNIVERSITY PRESS, MUSIC DEPARTMENT, 44 CONDUIT STREET, LONDON, W.1

Printed in Great Britain

O.U.P. 147

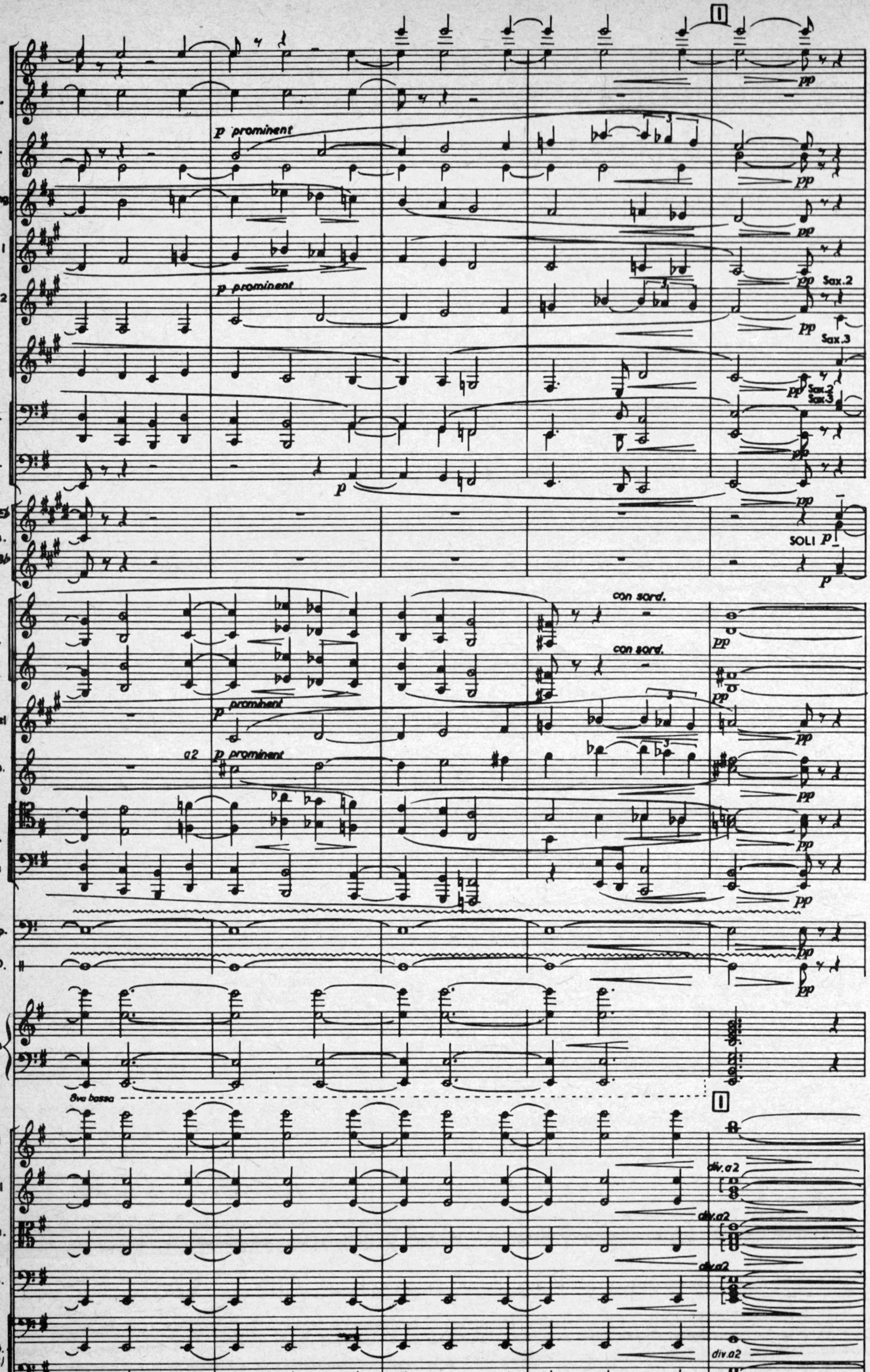
1
Fls.
Picc.
p prominent
Obs.
Cor. ang.
Cls.
1
2
p prominent
pp
Sax.2
Sax.3
B.Cl
Sax.2
Sax.3
Bns.
D.Bn.
1 2 E♭
Saxs.
3 B♭
SOLI
Hns.
con sord.
Flügel
prominent
Tpts.
a2
p prominent
Tbns.
Tuba
Timp.
B.D.
Harps
8va bassa
Vl. I
Vl. II
div. a2
Vla.
Vlc.
D.B.
(div.)

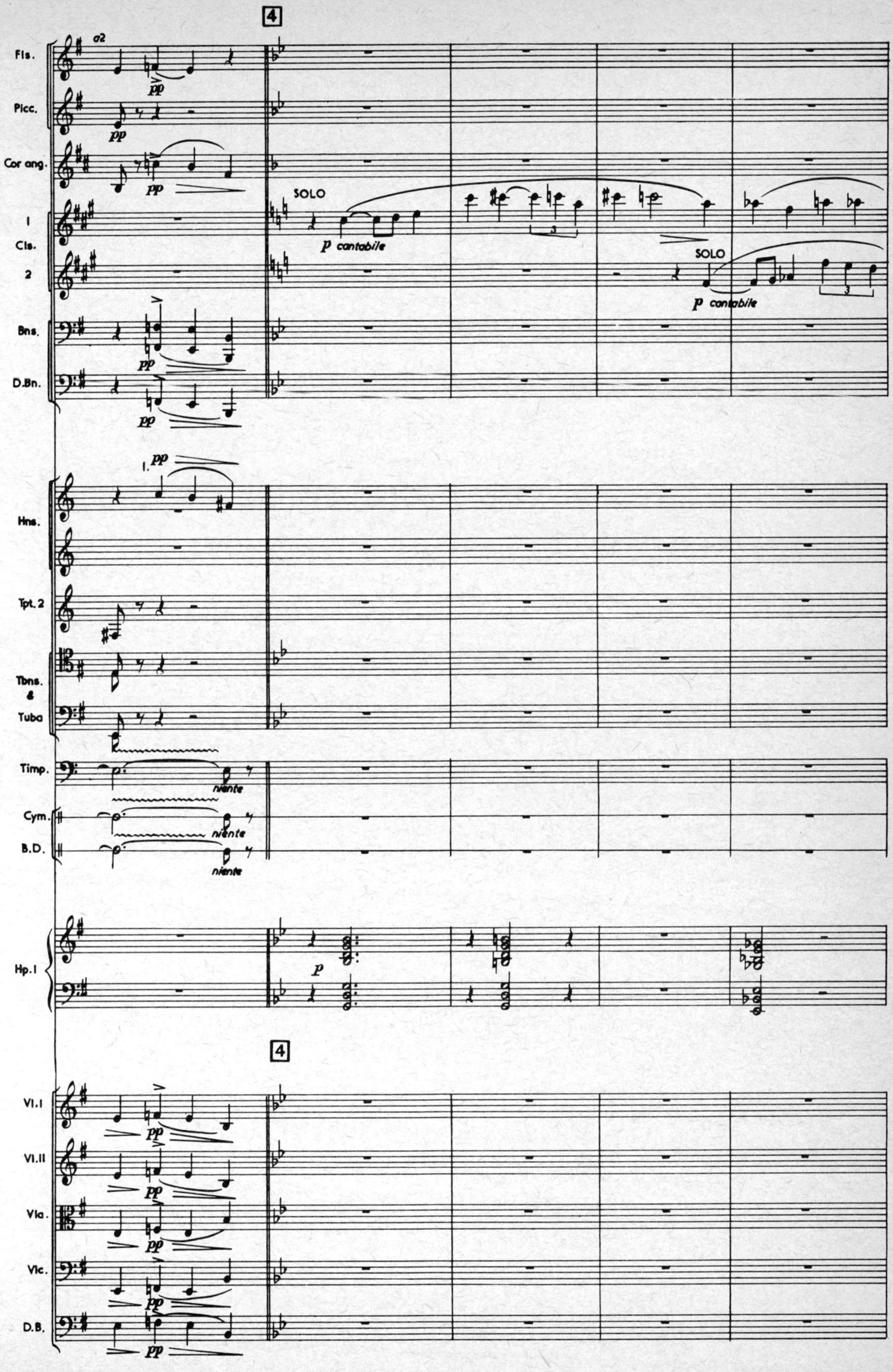
4
Fls.
a2
pp
Picc.
Cor ang.
SOLO
p cantabile
1
Cls.
2
Bns.
D.Bn.
1.
Hns.
Tpt. 2
Tbns. & Tuba
Timp.
niente
Cym.
B.D.
Hp. I
p
Vl. I
Vl. II
Vla.
Vlc.
D.B.

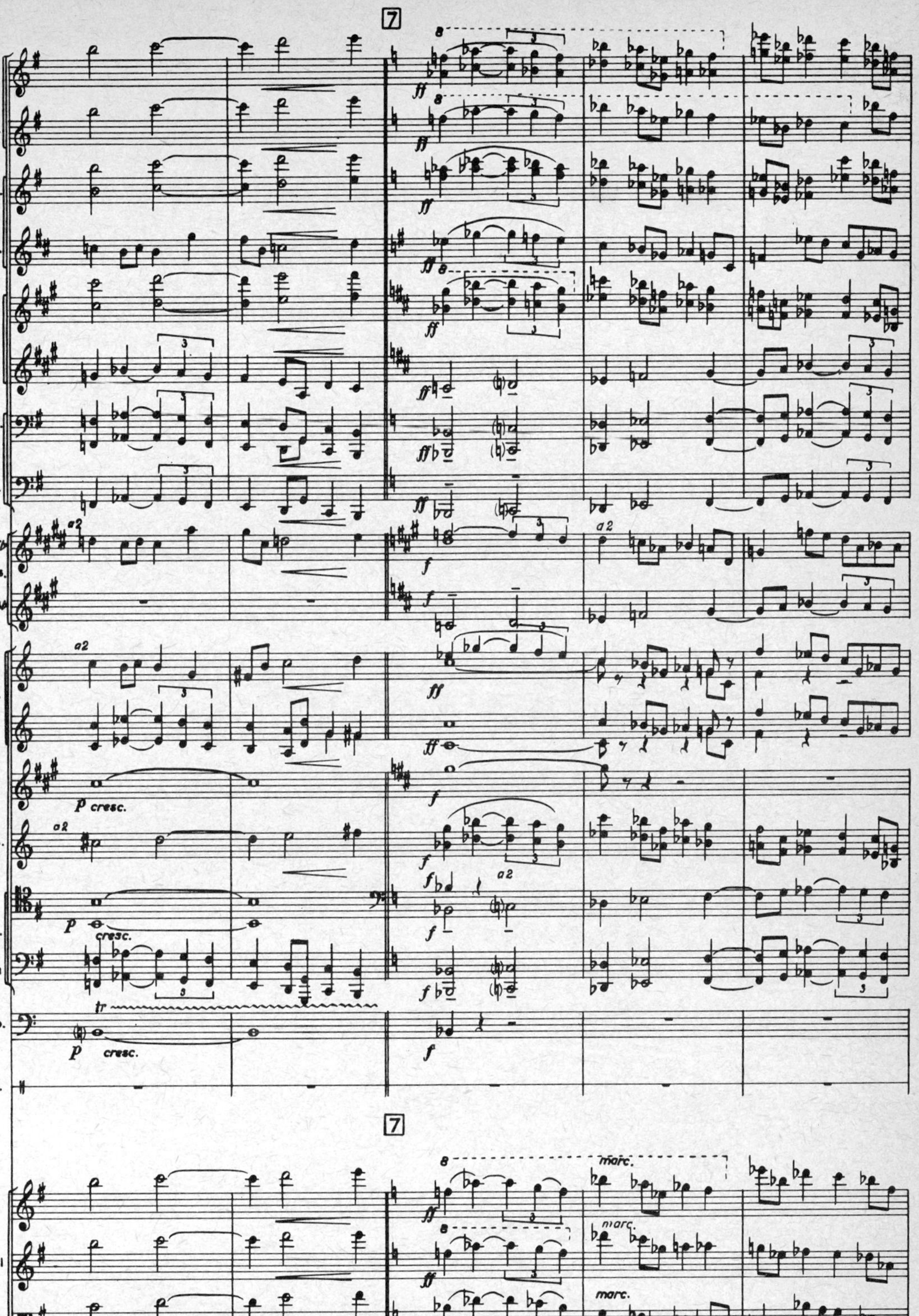
7
Fls.
Picc.
Obs.
Cor ang.
Cls.
B.Cl.
Bns.
D.Bn.
1.2 Eb
Saxs.
3 Bb
a2
Hns.
Flügel
p cresc.
Tpts.
Tbns.
&
Tuba
Timp.
tr
p cresc.
B.D.
7
Vl.I
Vl.II
Vla.
Vlc.
D.B.
marc.

14

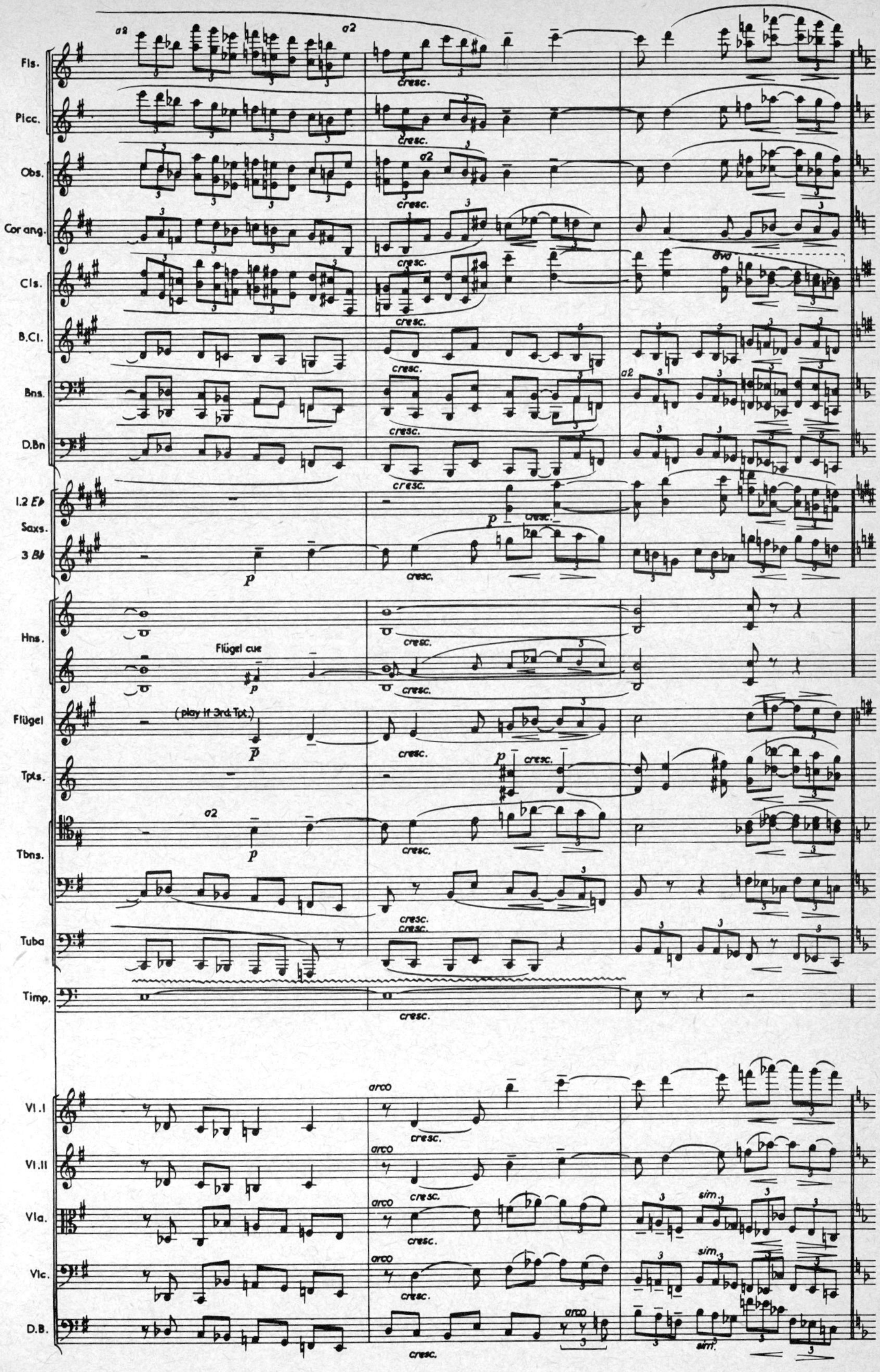
a2
a2
Fls.
Picc.
Obs.
Cor ang.
Cls.
B.Cl.
Bns.
D.Bn.
1.2 E♭
Saxs.
3 B♭
Hns.
Flügel cue
Flügel
(play if 3rd Tpt.)
Tpts.
Tbns.
Tuba
Timp.
Vl.I
Vl.II
Vla.
Vlc.
D.B.
cresc.
arco
sim.
8va
p

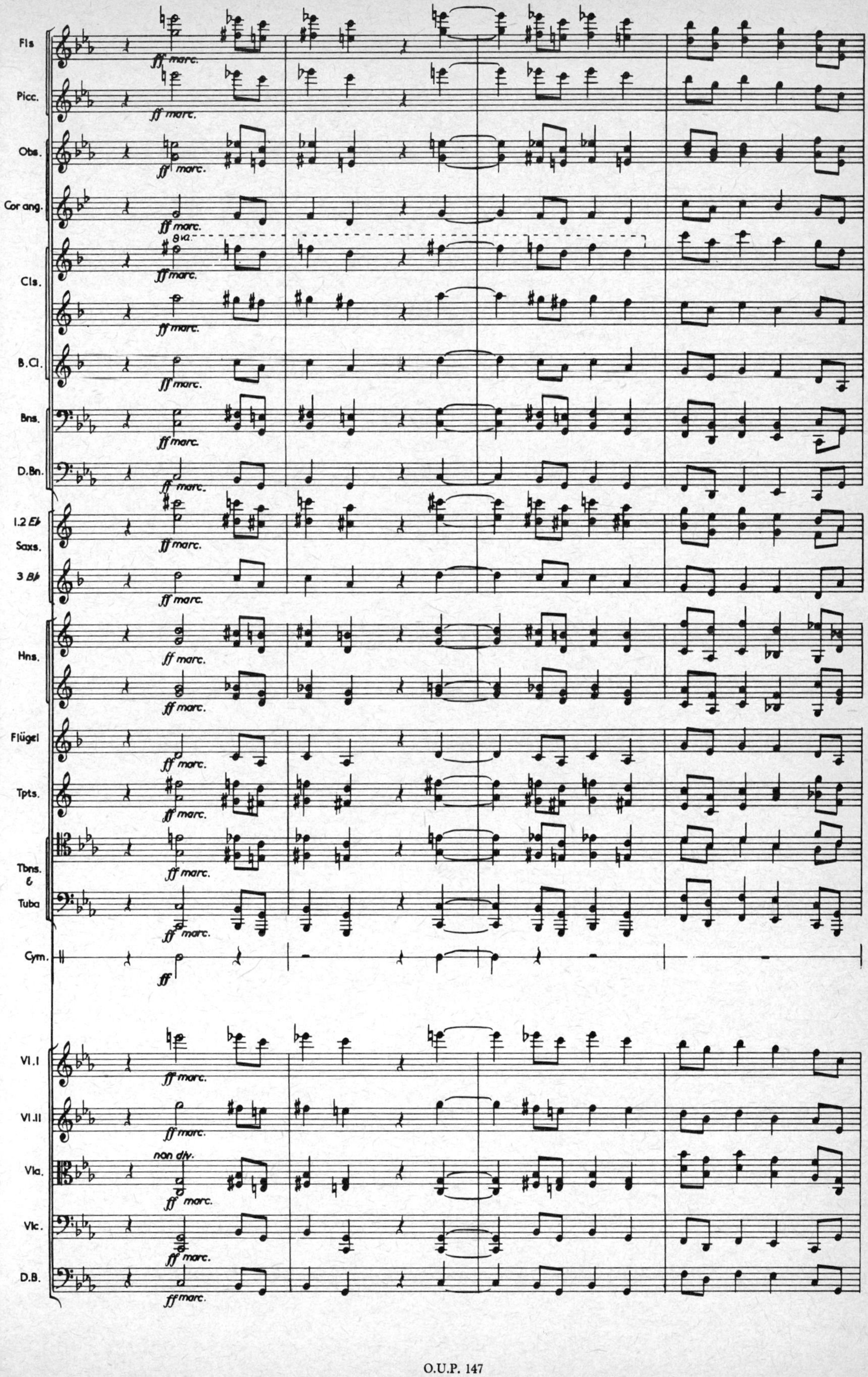
Fls
Picc.
Obs.
Cor ang.
Cls.
B. Cl.
Bns.
D. Bn.
1.2 E♭ Saxs.
3 B♭
Hns.
Flügel
Tpts.
Tbns. & Tuba
Cym.
Vl. I
Vl. II
Vla.
Vlc.
D.B.
ff marc.
8va
non div.
ff

25
26
Fls. 1 2
Obs.
Cor ang.
Cls.
B. Cl.
Bns.
Sax. 2 cue
Sax. 3 cue
1,2 E♭ Saxs. 3 B♭
Hns.
con sord.
Flügel
Flügel cue
Tpt. 1
Tbns. 1 3
Hp. 1
Vl. I
Vl. II
Vla.
Vlc.
D.B
div. a2
p
pp
ppp

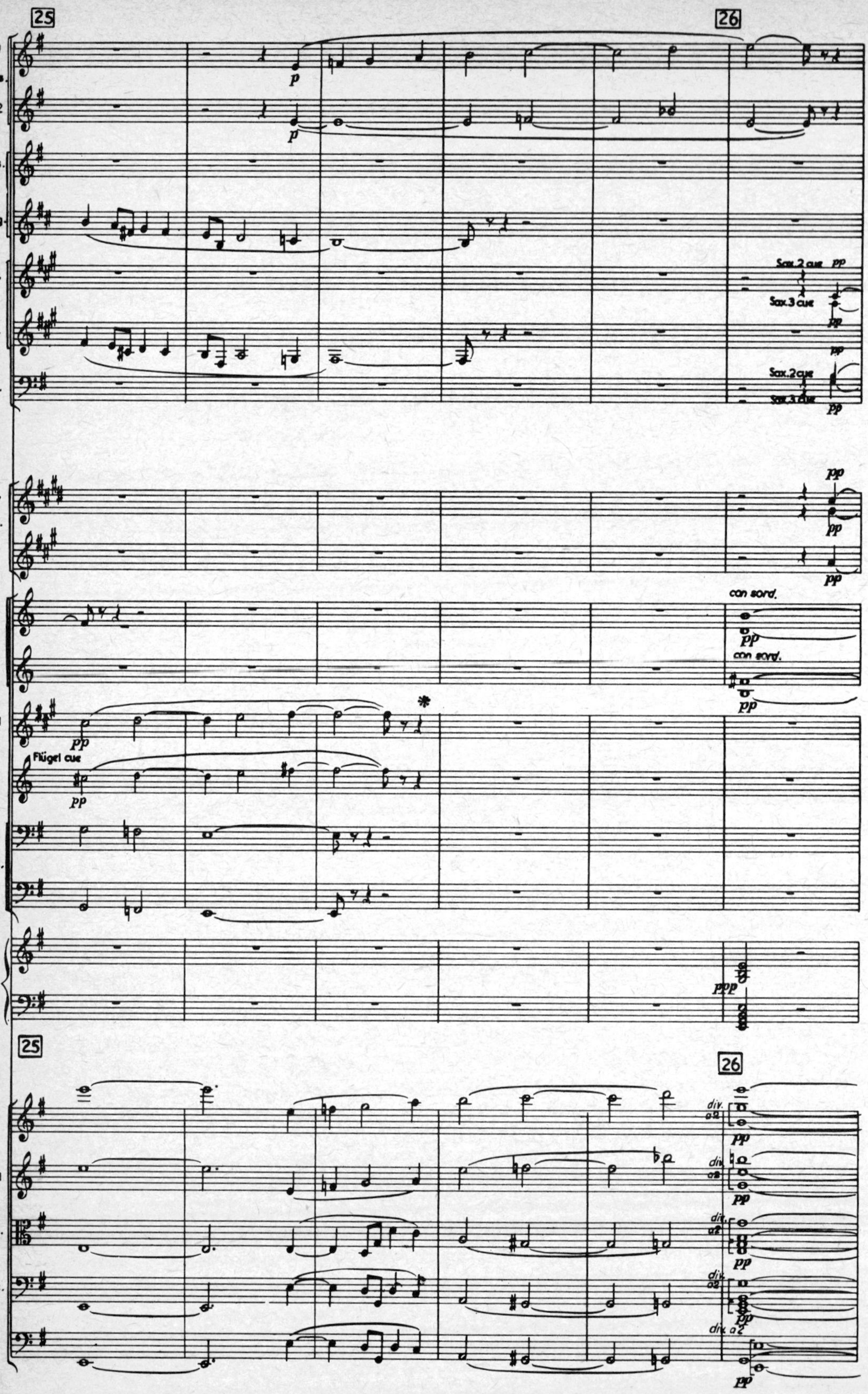

II

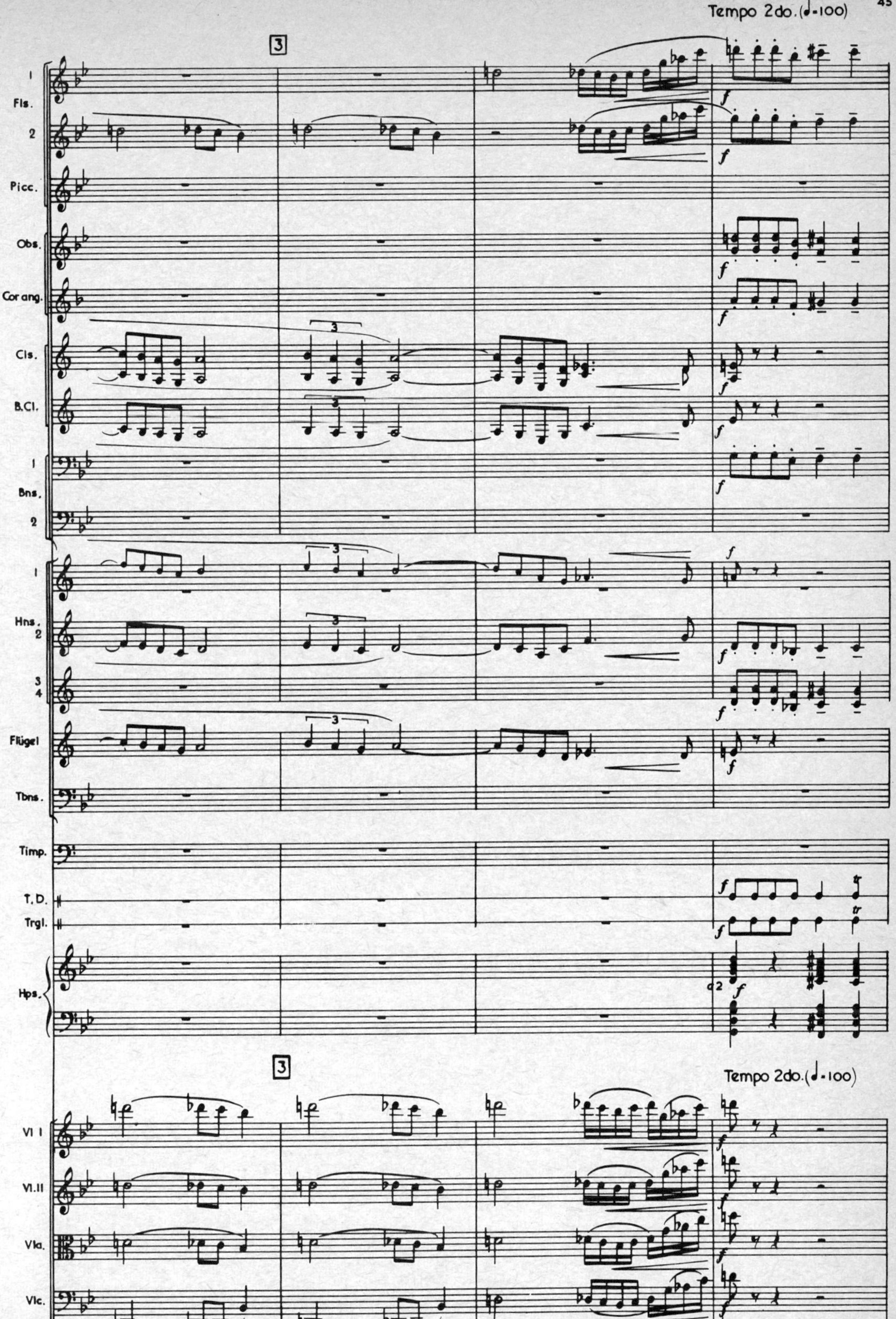
Tempo 2do. (𝅗𝅥=100)
3
1
Fls.
2
Picc.
Obs.
Cor ang.
3
Cls.
B.Cl.
1
Bns.
2
1
3
Hns.
2
3
4
3
Flügel
Tbns.
Timp.
T. D.
Trgl.
Hps.
3
Tempo 2do. (𝅗𝅥=100)
Vl I
Vl. II
Vla.
Vlc.
D.B.

48

O.U.P. 147

O.U.P. 147

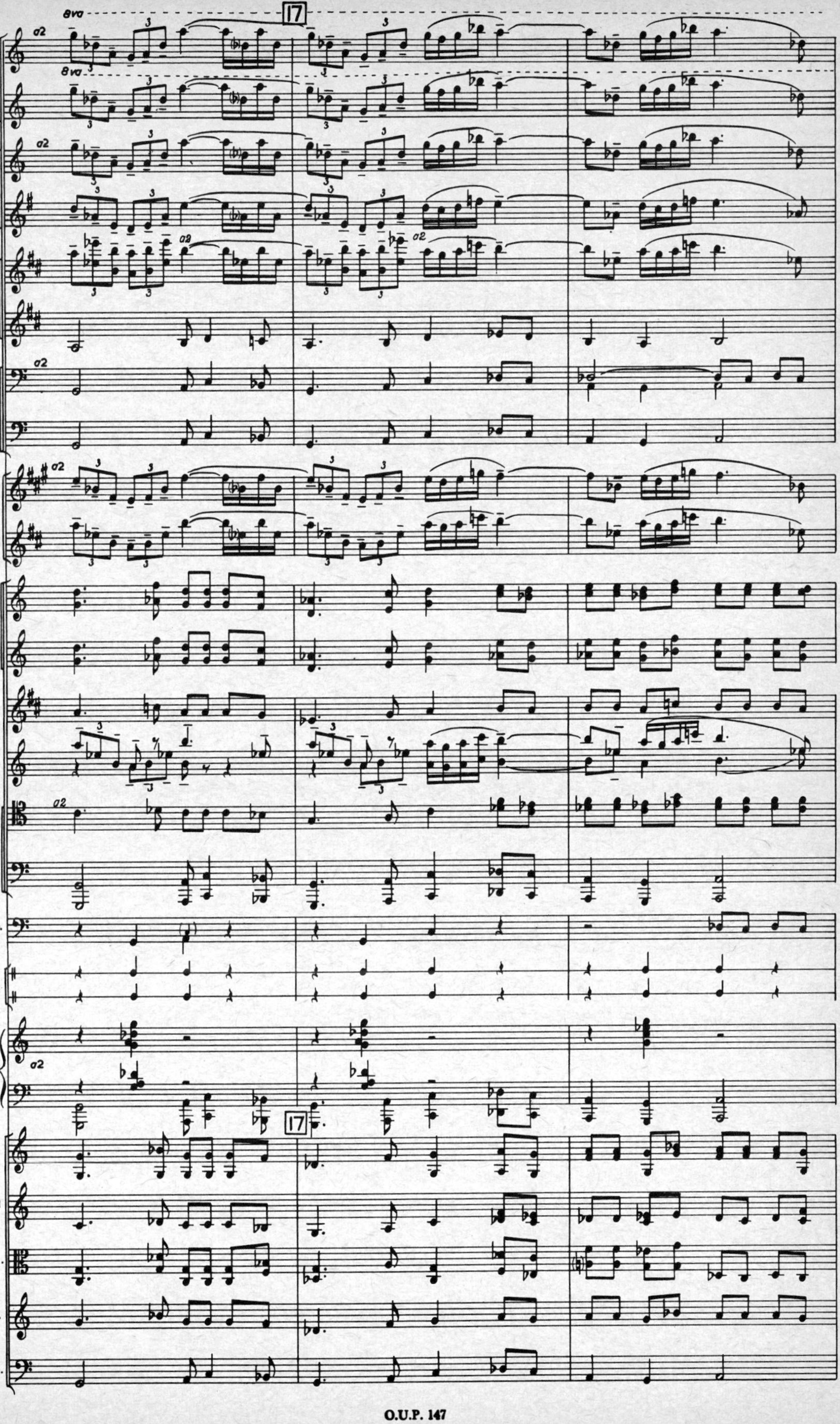
17
Fls.
Picc.
Obs
Cor ang.
Cls
B. Cl
Bns.
D. Bn.
1.2 E♭ Saxs
3 B♭
Hns.
Flügel
Tpts.
Tbns. & Tuba
Timp.
Cym.
B. D
Hps.
Vl. I
Vl. II
Vla.
Vlc.
D.B.

22 Tempo I mo. (♩=76)
Fls.
Obs.
pp
Cls.
SOLO
p cantabile
B.Cl.
Bns.
Hn. I
Flügel
Flügel cue
p cantabile
*→TACET IF 3RD. TPT.
SOLO
p cantabile
Hp. I
22 Tempo I mo. (♩=76)
Vl I
unis.
div.
pp
Vl.II
pp
Vla.
pp
SOLO
ppp
Vlc.
pp
TUTTI
div.
pp
D.B.
pp

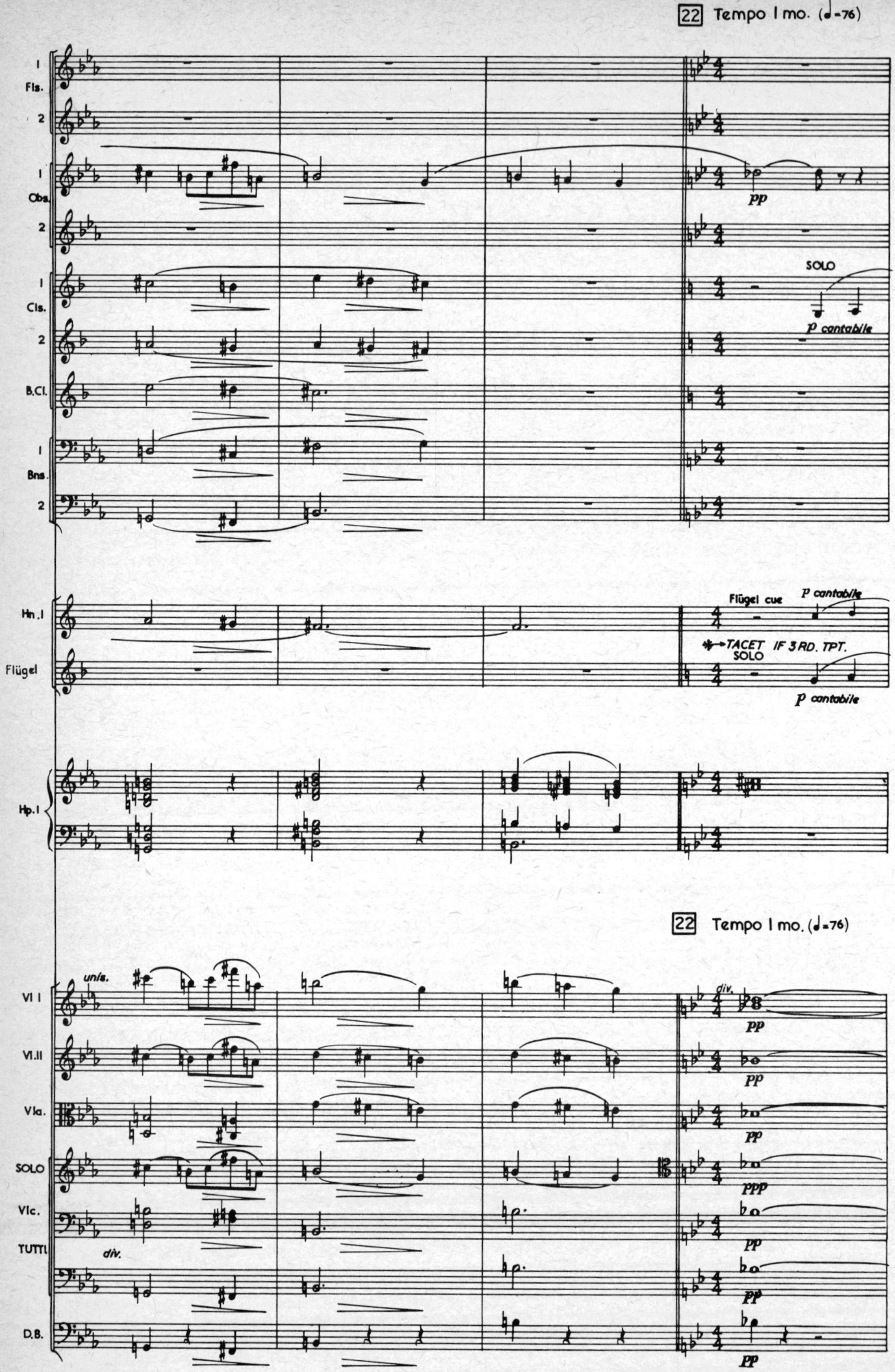

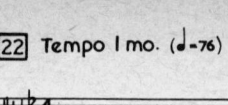

III SCHERZO

74

76

O.U.P. 147

O.U.P. 147

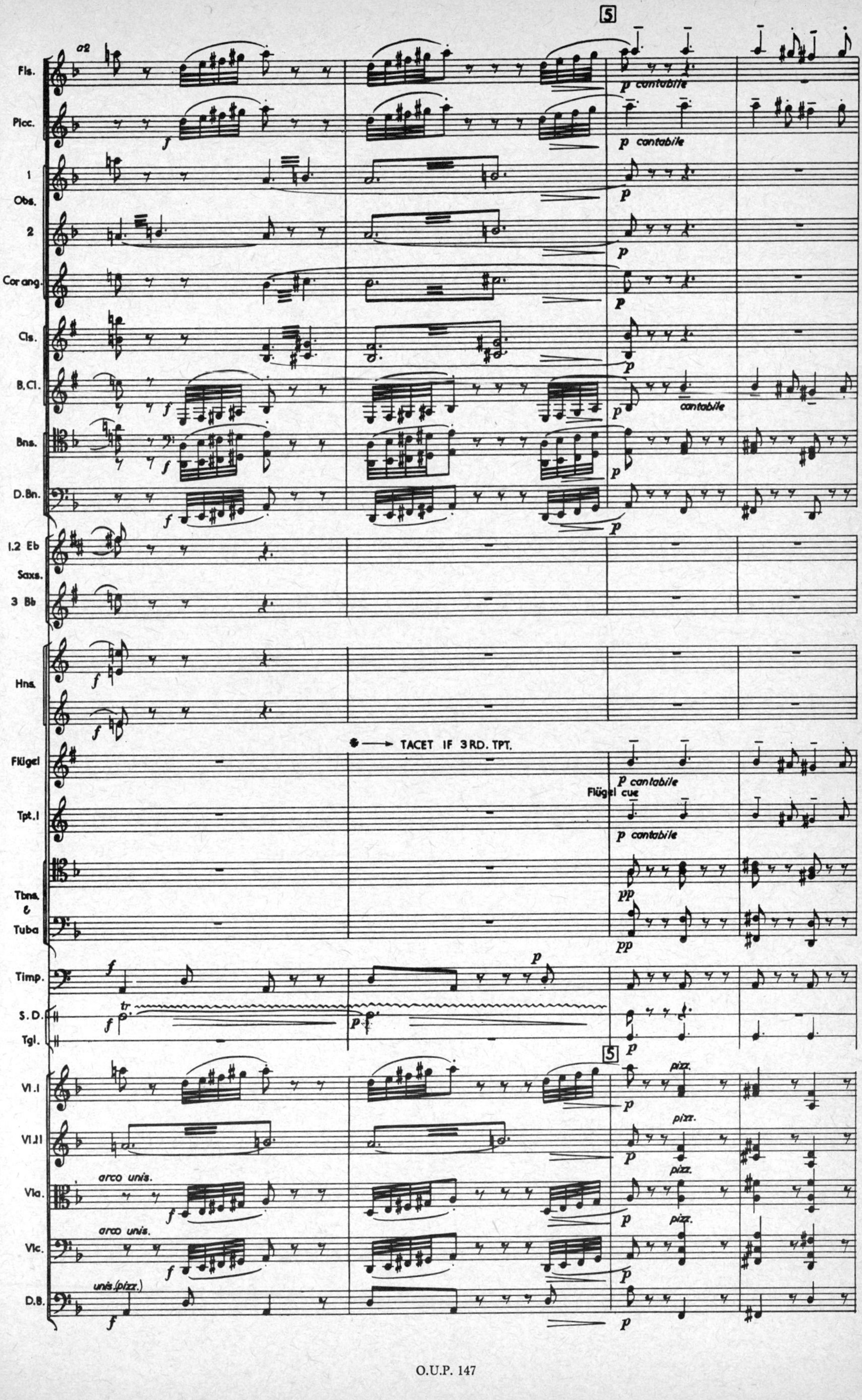
5
a2
Fls.
Picc.
1
Obs.
2
Cor ang.
Cls.
B. Cl.
Bns.
D. Bn.
1.2 Eb
Saxs.
3 Bb
Hns.
Flügel
Tpt. I
Tbns. & Tuba
Timp.
S. D.
Tgl.
Vl. I
Vl. II
Vla.
Vlc.
D.B.
p cantabile
cantabile
TACET IF 3RD. TPT.
Flügel cue
tr
pizz.
arco unis.
unis.(pizz.)

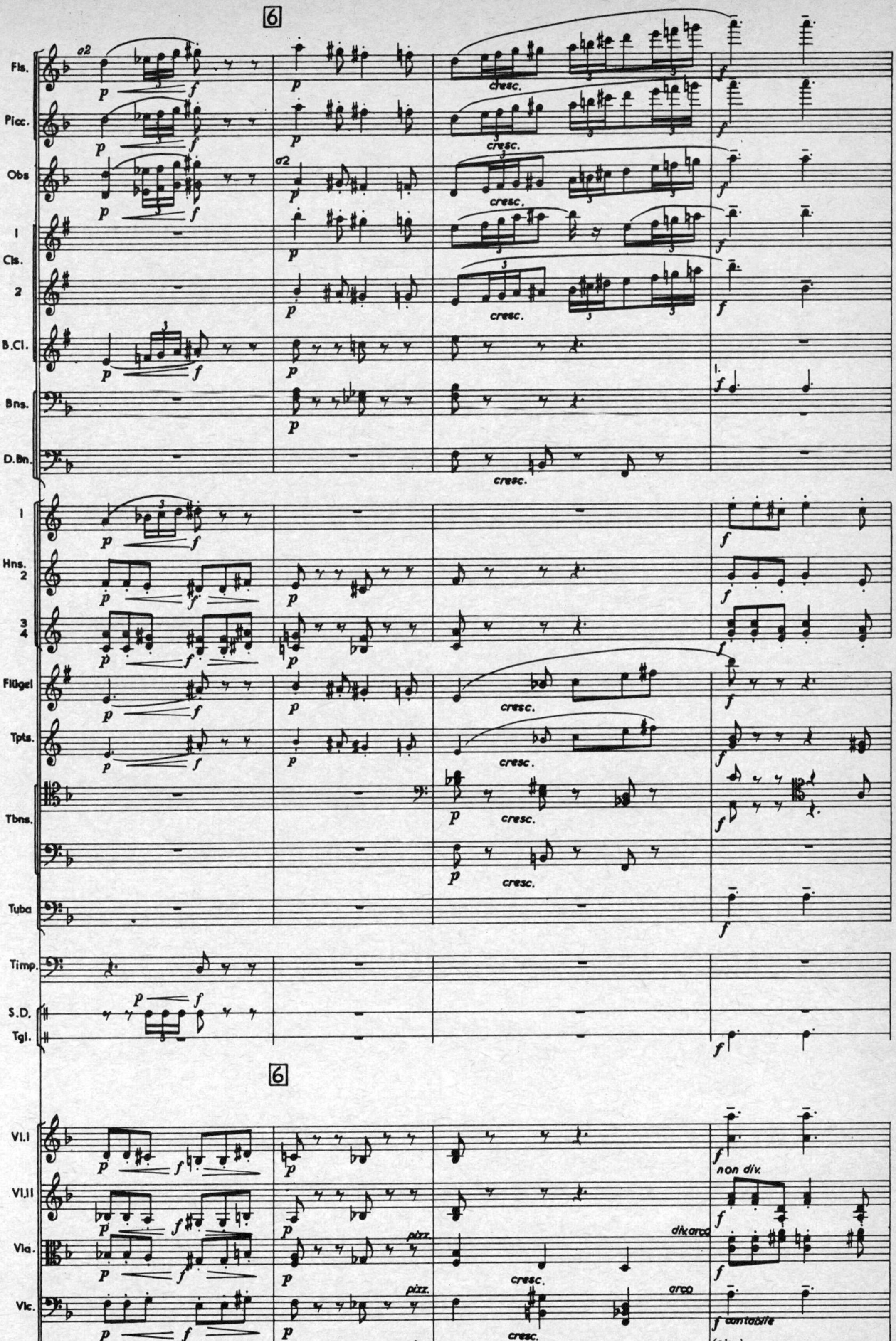
6
Fls.
Picc.
Obs
1
Cls.
2
B.Cl.
Bns.
D.Bn.
1
Hns. 2
3 4
Flügel
Tpts.
Tbns.
Tuba
Timp.
S.D.
Tgl.
6
Vl.I
Vl.II
Vla.
Vlc.
D.B.
cresc.
pizz.
non div.
div.arco
arco
f cantabile
(pizz.)

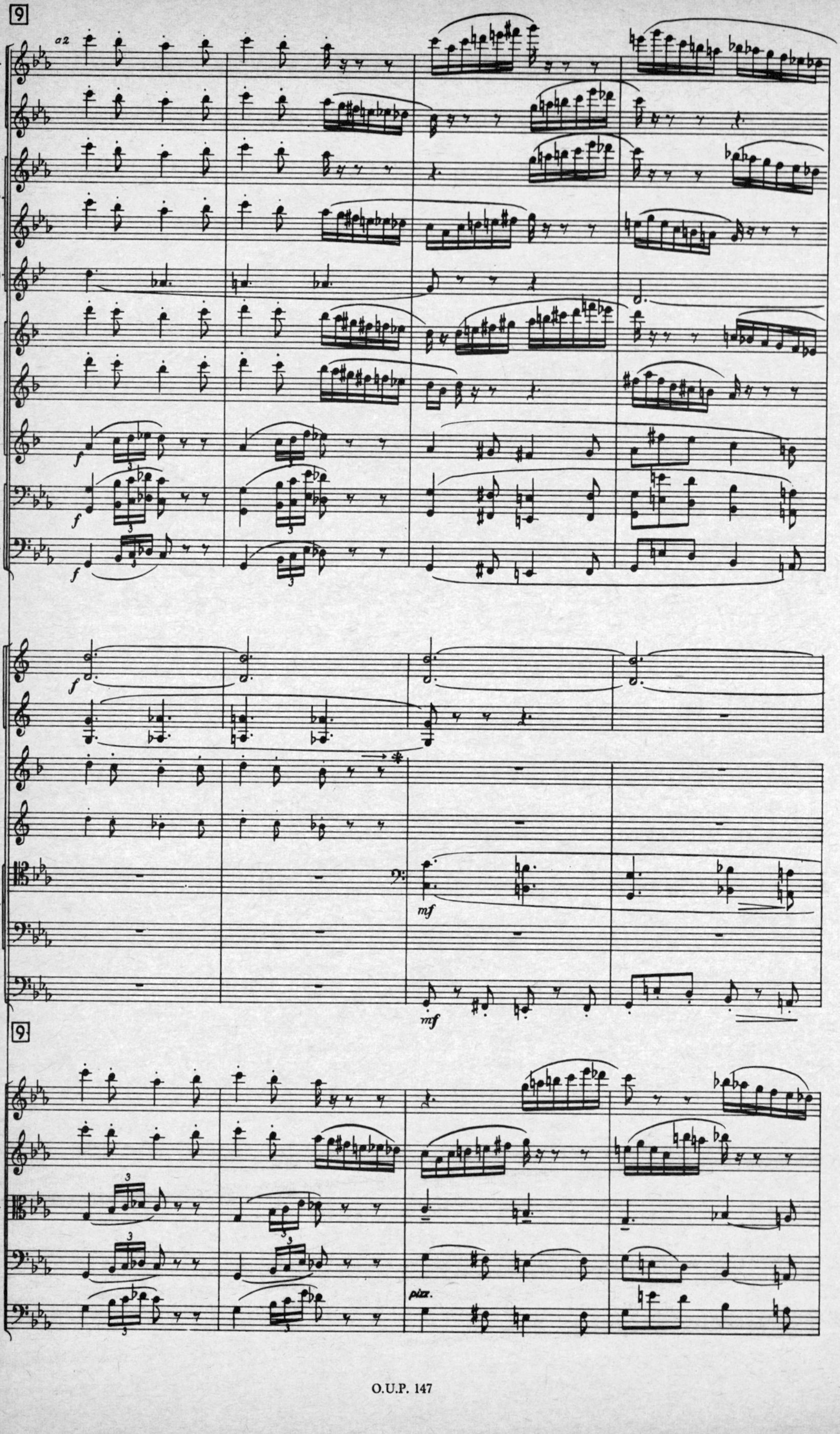
9
a2
Fls.
Picc.
Obs.
Cor ang.
Cls.
B.Cl.
Bns.
D.Bn.
Hns.
Flügel
Tpt.I
Tbns.
Tuba
9
Vl.I
Vl.II
Vla.
Vlc.
D.B.
pizz.

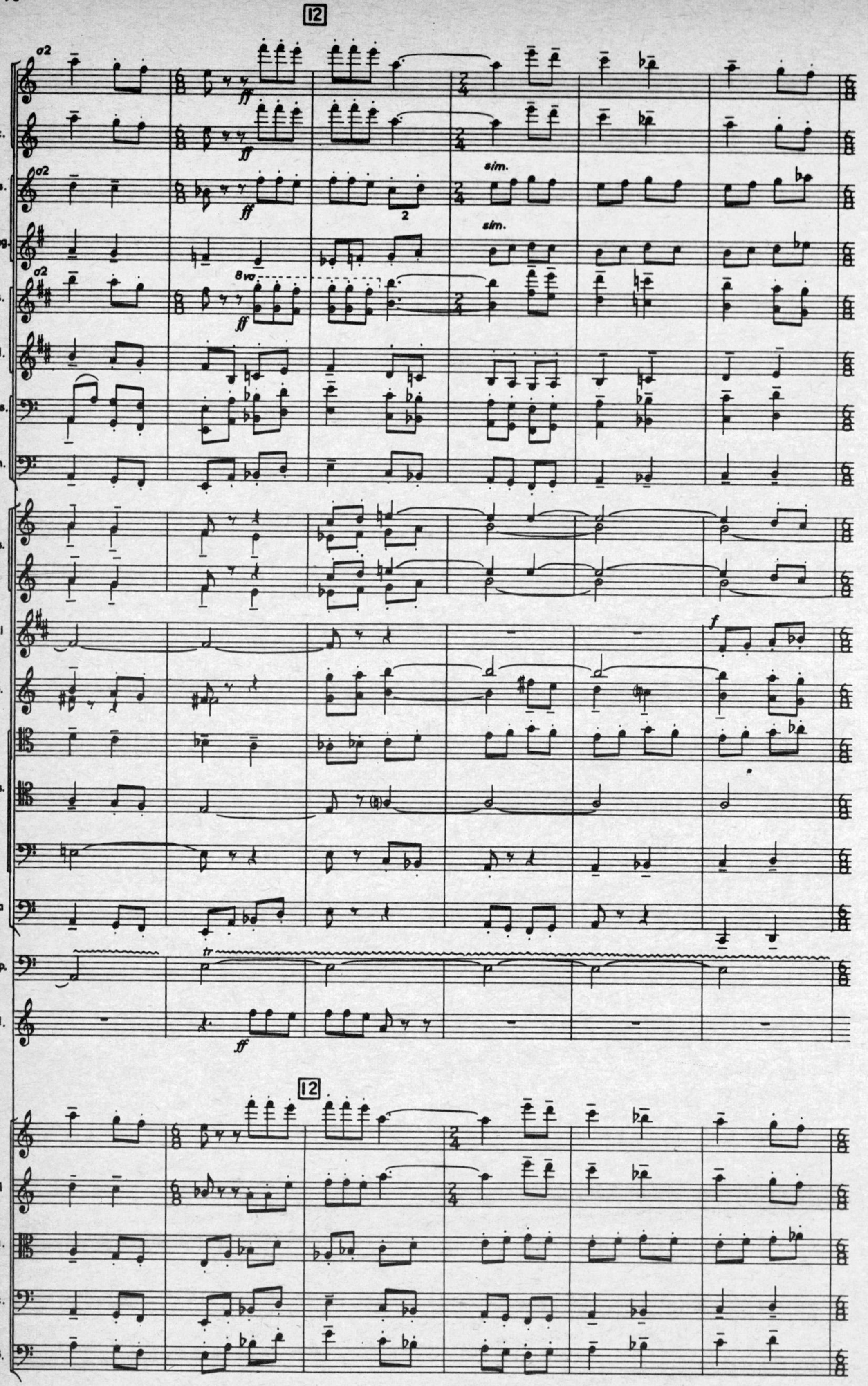
12
Fls.
Picc.
Obs.
Cor.ang.
Cls.
B.Cl.
Bns.
D.Bn.
Hns.
Flügel
Tpts.
Tbns.
Tuba
Timp.
Xyl.
Vl.I
Vl.II
Vla.
Vlc.
D.B.
ff
sim.
8va
tr
f

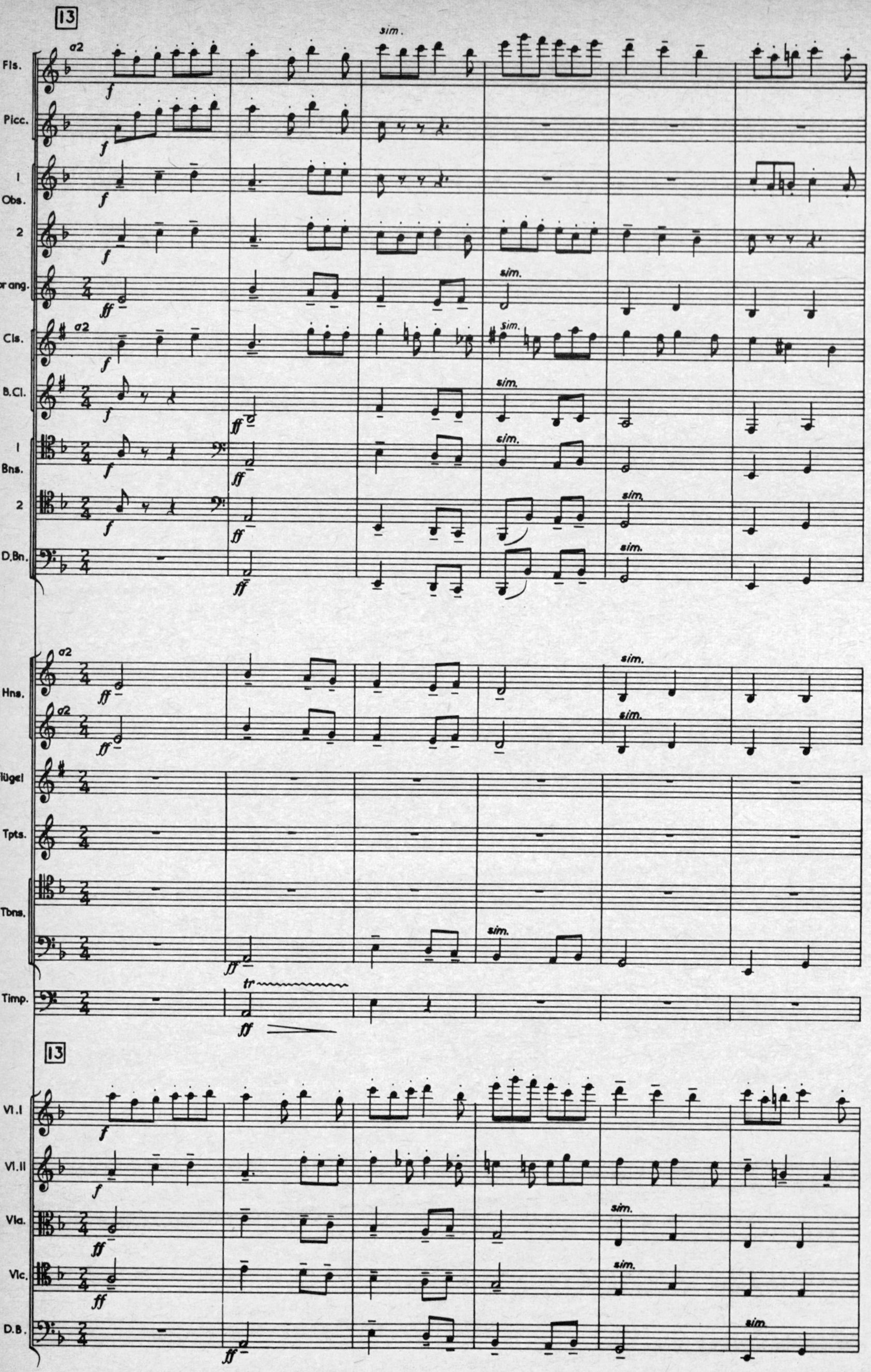
13
Fls.
Picc.
1
Obs.
2
Cor ang.
Cls.
B.Cl.
1
Bns.
2
D.Bn.
Hns.
Flügel
Tpts.
Tbns.
Timp.
13
Vl.I
Vl.II
Vla.
Vlc.
D.B.
a2
sim.
f
ff
tr

98

O.U.P. 147

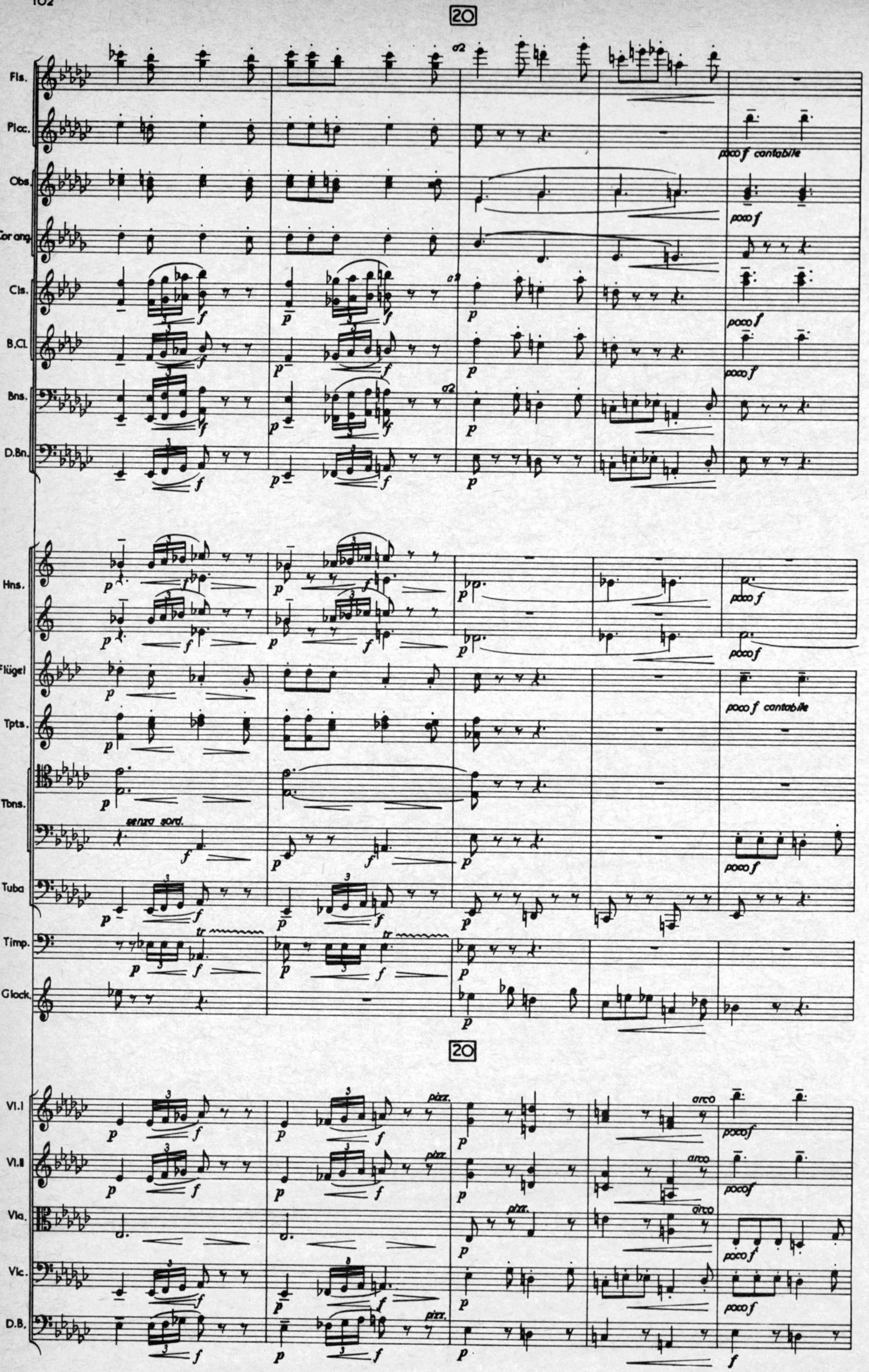
20
Fls.
Picc.
poco f cantabile
Obs.
poco f
Cor ang.
Cls.
poco f
B.Cl.
poco f
Bns.
D.Bn.
Hns.
poco f
Flügel
poco f cantabile
Tpts.
Tbns.
senza sord.
poco f
Tuba
Timp.
tr
Glock.
20
Vl.I
pizz.
arco
poco f
Vl.II
Vla.
D.B.
Vlc.

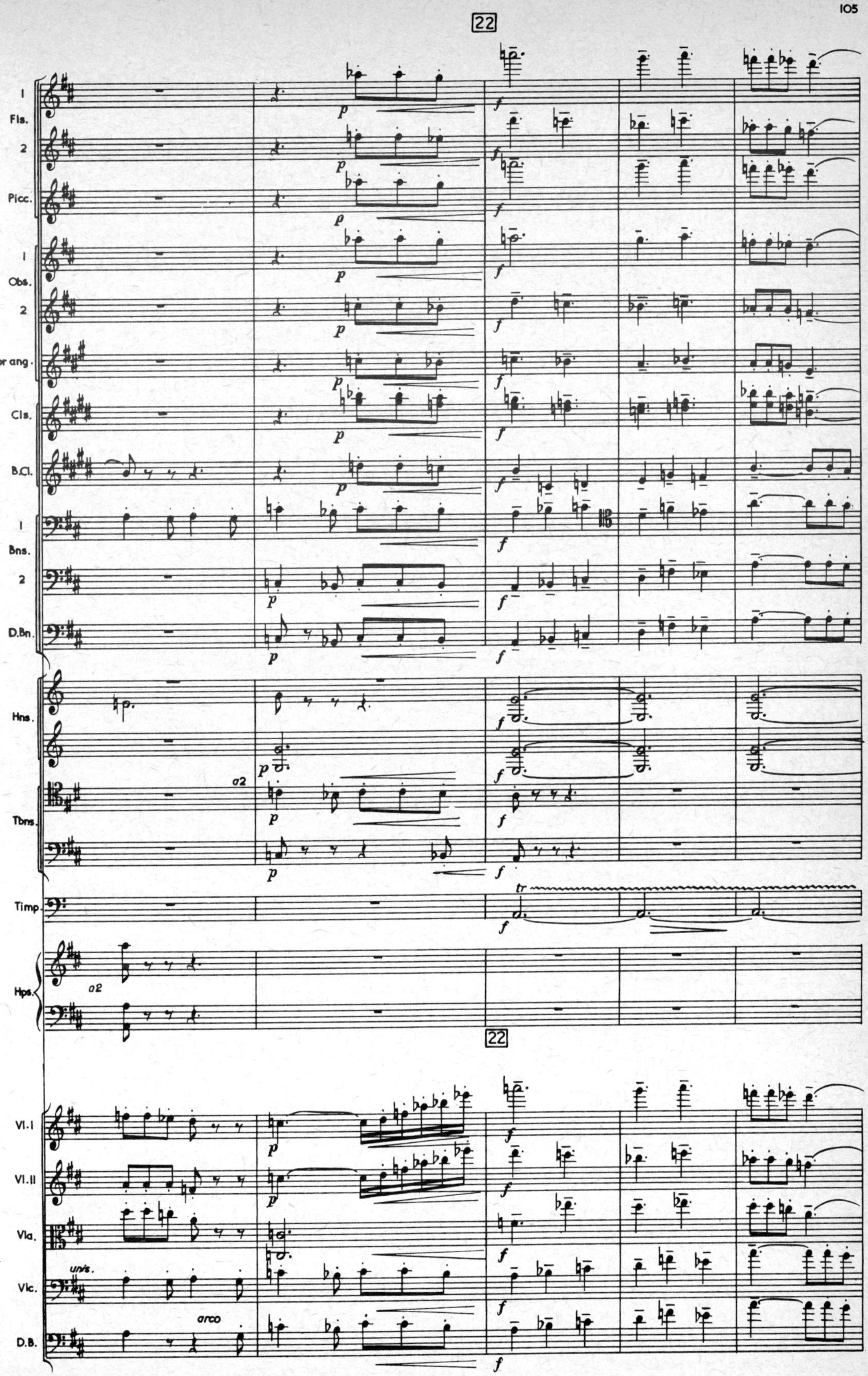
22
Fls.
Picc.
Obs.
Cor ang.
Cls.
B.Cl.
Bns.
D.Bn.
Hns.
Tbns.
a2
Timp.
tr
Hps.
a2
22
Vl.I
Vl.II
Vla.
unis.
Vlc.
arco
D.B.

O.U.P. 147

NOTE: The wait before No. IV should be about the value of three bars of No. III.

[The Orchestration for this movement is the same as that of the others]

IV

Andante tranquillo (♩.=60)

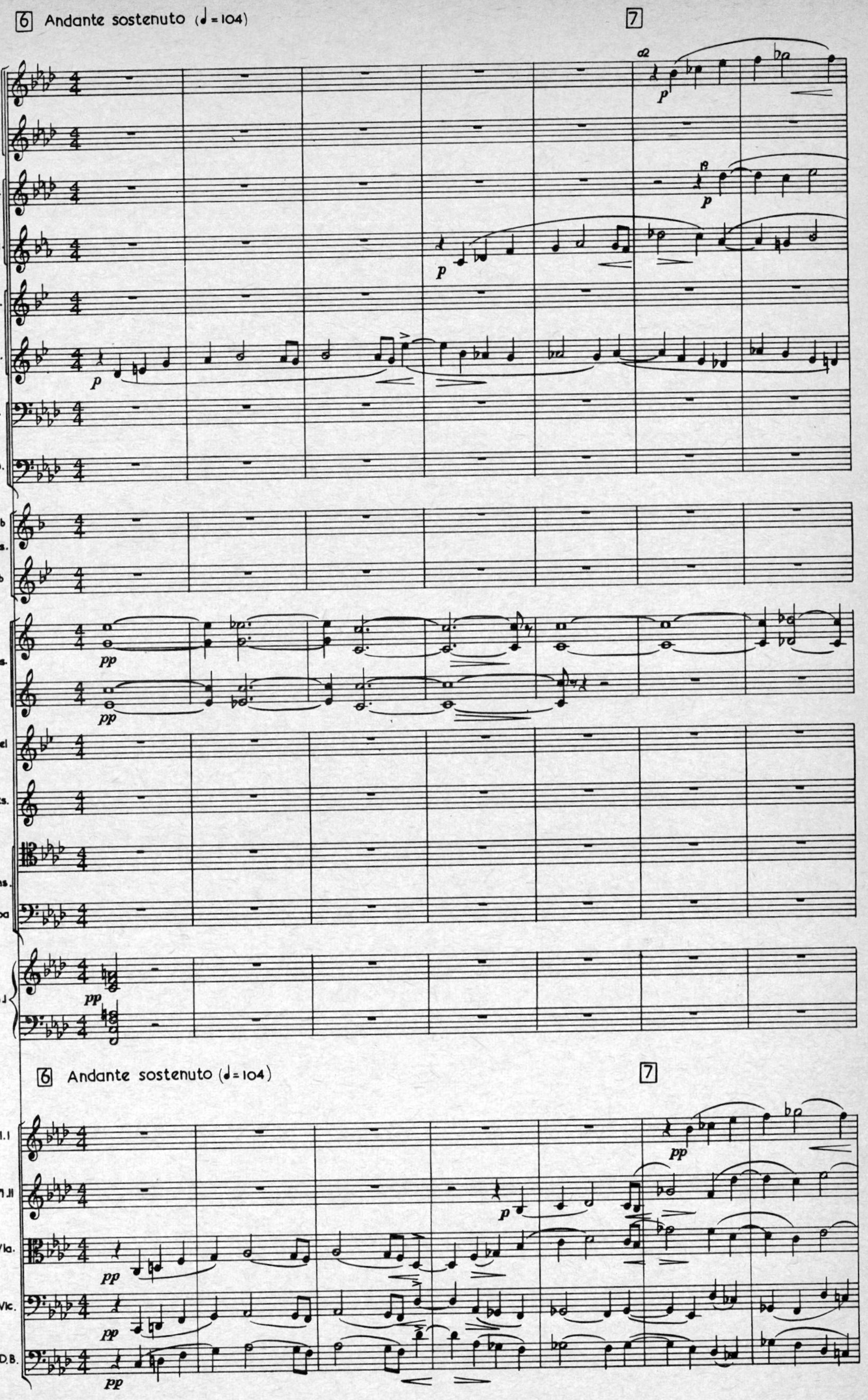
6 Andante sostenuto (♩= 104)
7
Fls.
Picc.
Obs.
Cor ang.
Cls.
B.Cl.
Bns.
D.Bn.
1.2 Eb Saxs.
3 Bb
Hns.
Flügel
Tpts.
Tbns. & Tuba
Hp.I
6 Andante sostenuto (♩= 104)
7
Vl.I
Vl.II
Vla.
Vlc.
D.B.
a2
p
pp

140

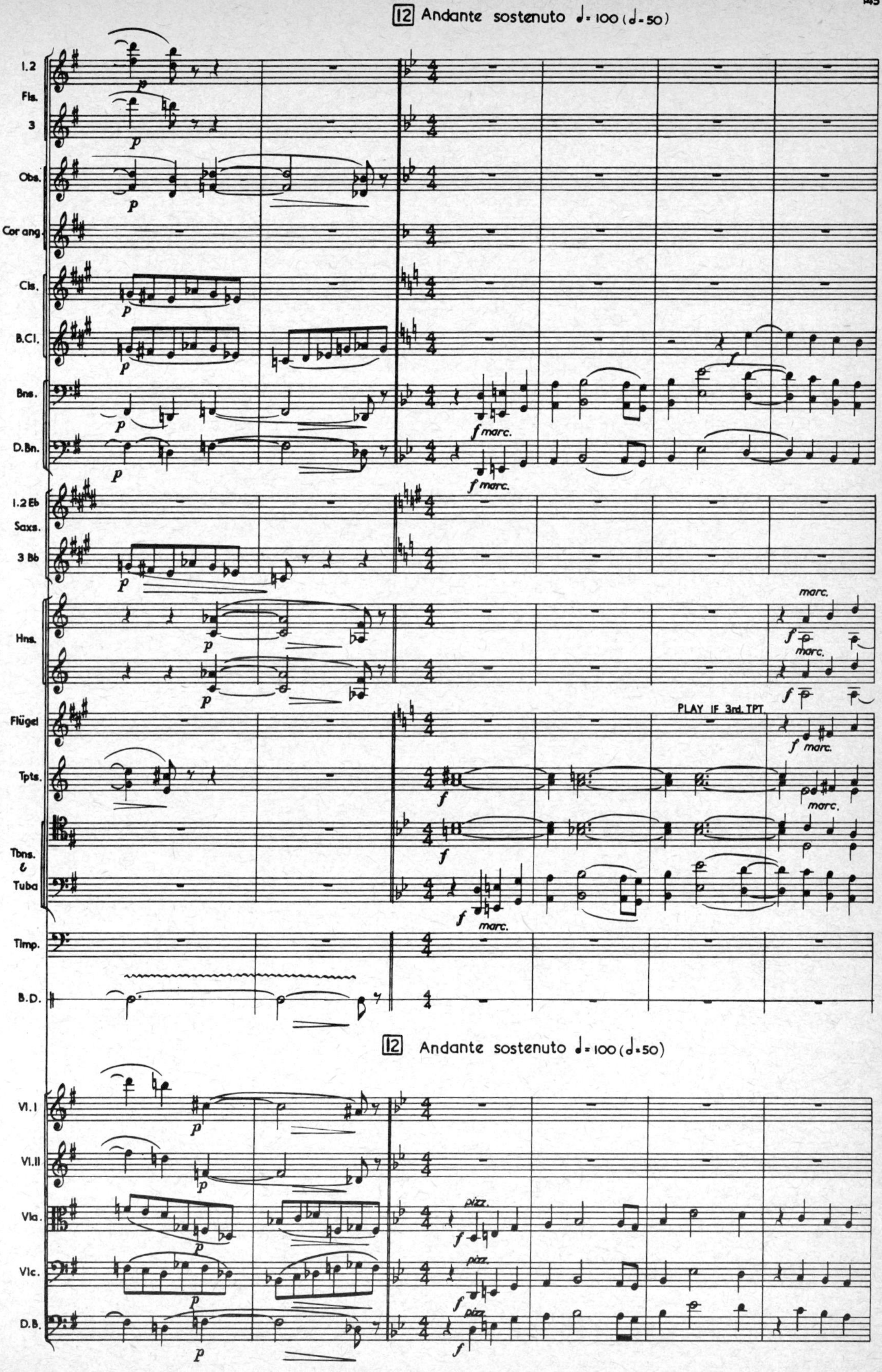
12 Andante sostenuto ♩= 100 (𝅗𝅥= 50)
1.2 Fls. 3
Obs.
Cor ang.
Cls.
B.Cl.
Bns.
D.Bn.
1.2 Eb Saxs. 3 Bb
Hns.
Flügel
Tpts.
Tbns. & Tuba
Timp.
B.D.
p
f marc.
marc.
PLAY IF 3rd. TPT.
f
12 Andante sostenuto ♩= 100 (𝅗𝅥= 50)
Vl. I
Vl. II
Vla.
Vlc.
D.B.
pizz.

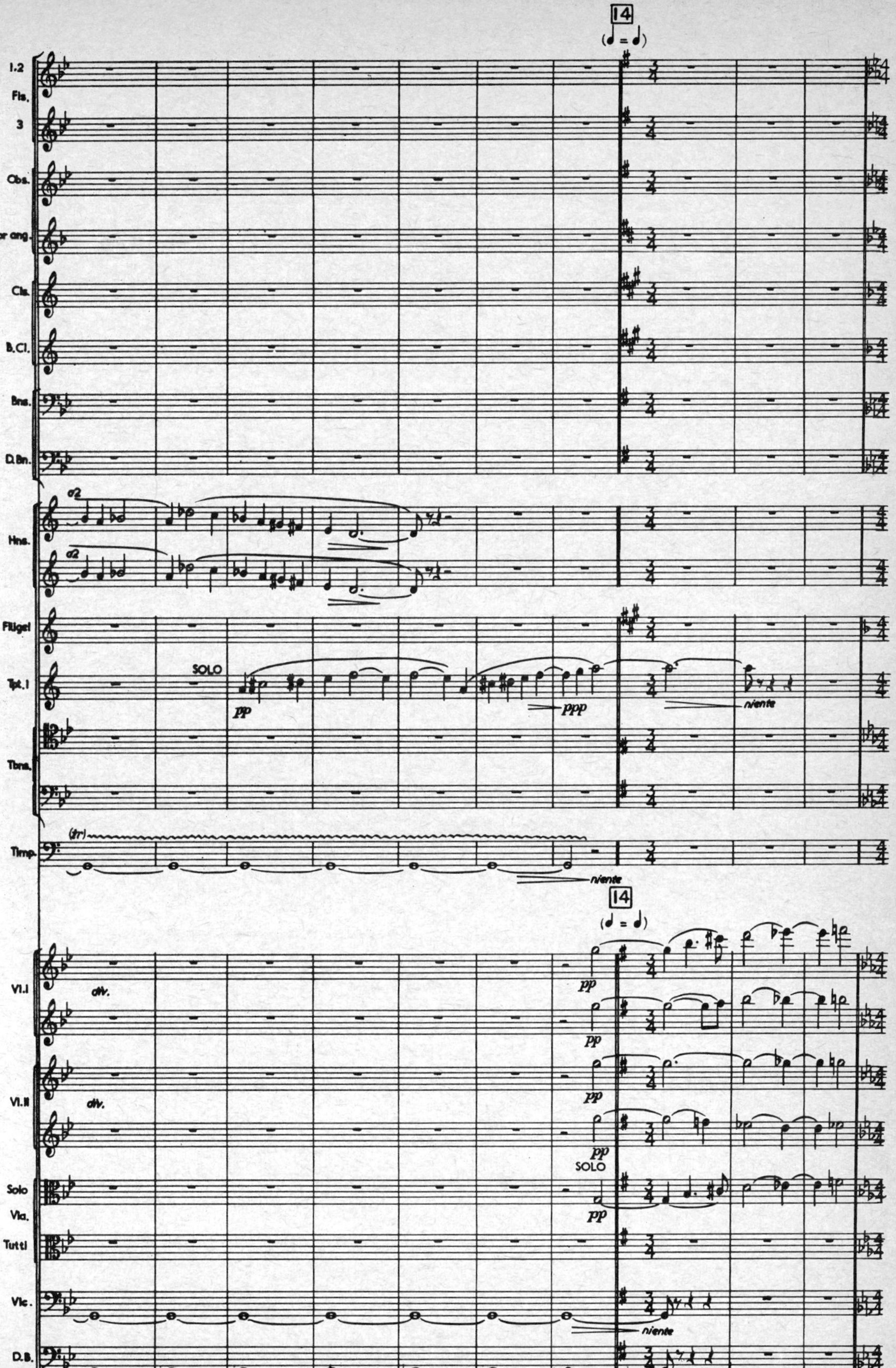
14
(♩ = ♩)
1.2
Fls.
3
Obs.
Cor ang.
Cls.
B.Cl.
Bns.
D.Bn.
Hns.
Flügel
Tpt. I
SOLO
pp
ppp
niente
Tbns.
Timp.
(tr)
niente
14
(♩ = ♩)
Vl. I
div.
pp
Vl. II
div.
pp
SOLO
Solo
Vla.
Tutti
pp
Vlc.
niente
D.B.
niente

148

NOTE: The composer made a small cut in this work before publication and, as a result, rehearsal figure 15 is omitted.

O.U.P. 147

153

O.U.P. 147

154

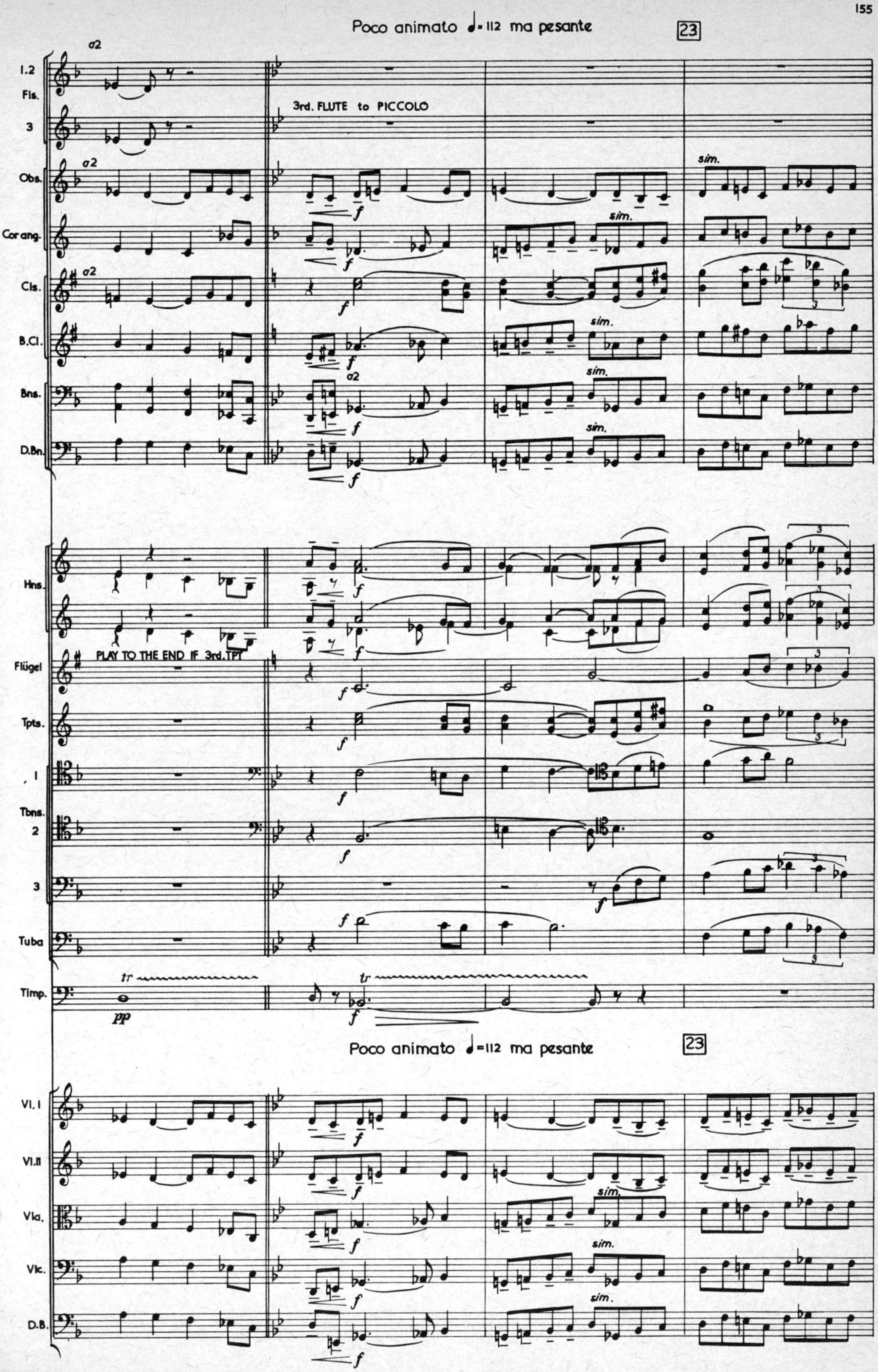
Poco animato 𝅗𝅥=112 ma pesante
23
a2
1.2 Fls.
3
3rd. FLUTE to PICCOLO
Obs.
Cor ang.
Cls.
B.Cl.
Bns.
D.Bn.
sim.
Hns.
Flügel
PLAY TO THE END IF 3rd. TPT
Tpts.
Tbns.
Tuba
Timp.
tr
pp
f
Poco animato 𝅗𝅥=112 ma pesante
23
Vl. I
Vl. II
Vla.
Vlc.
D.B.

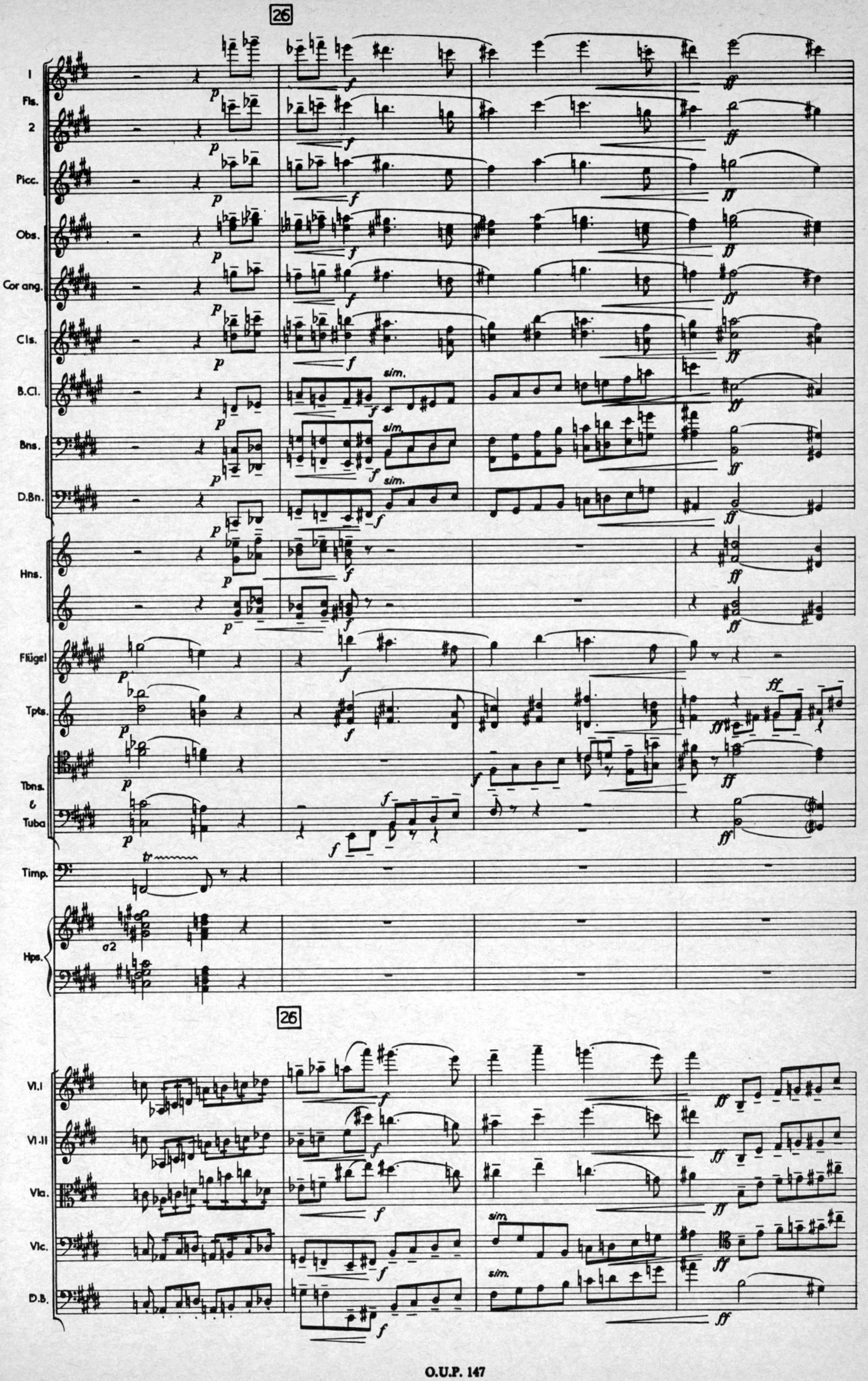
26
Fls. 1 2
Picc.
Obs.
Cor ang.
Cls.
B.Cl.
Bns.
D.Bn.
Hns.
Flügel
Tpts.
Tbns. & Tuba
Timp.
Hps.
a2
sim.
p
f
ff
tr
26
Vl. I
Vl. II
Vla.
Vlc.
D.B.